I0116824

Instant Insights on...

How to Sit & Stay with Compassionate Meditation

SABRINA JOHNSON

Crescendo
PUBLISHING

Instant Insights on...

How to Sit & Stay with Compassionate Meditation
By Sabrina Johnson, RScP

Copyright © 2017 by Sabrina Johnson, RScP

All rights reserved. No part of this publication may be reproduced, distributed, or transmitted in any form or by any means, including photocopying, recording, or other electronic or mechanical methods, or by any information storage and retrieval system, without the prior written permission of the publisher and author, except in the case of brief quotations embodied in critical reviews and certain other non-commercial uses permitted by copyright law.

Crescendo Publishing, LLC
300 Carlsbad Village Drive
Ste. 108A, #443
Carlsbad, California 92008-2999

www.CrescendoPublishing.com

GetPublished@CrescendoPublishing.com
1-877-575-8814

ISBN: 978-1-944177-76-8 (P)
ISBN: 978-1-944177-77-5 (E)

Printed in the United States of America
Cover design by Melody Hunter

10 9 8 7 6 5 4 3 2 1

What You'll Learn in this Book

This book is for you if you have never meditated before and want to start. This book is for you if you've been meditating for many years and are curious to learn more. This book is for you if you have only a passing interest in meditation, but the title intrigued you enough to buy it. Because although this book is about meditation, it's truly about living from the heart. But to live from the heart, we have to be fully present, and mindfulness meditation teaches us how to be present. This book gives you some mindfulness meditation guidelines and teaches you how to easily integrate them into your life.

This book also acts as a looking glass that you can peer into so that once you become more mindfully present, you can also be heartfully present. But heartfulness is not something anyone else can teach you. You can only teach yourself as you learn. Every one of us already has the basics with which to start the process—an immeasurable capacity to love, to be loved, and to be loving. But if we don't give ourselves the time and space to focus our attention on these heart's desires, then they can't develop and expand. We realize their fulfillment when we are totally in the here and now.

It was only after I learned how to meditate that I became aware of how much time I spent not being present, and how that closed off my heart. This is my story that I share with you, not as an expert or authority, but as someone still very much on the learning curve. And oh! Is it ever a joyride!

One thing I've learned is that our furry, four-legged loved ones are masters at living in the moment, at living from the heart. They demonstrate this when they comfort us by being totally present, somehow innately knowing there is nothing to do but sit and stay -- and perhaps give a sloppy, wet kiss. And when they obey our command to sit and stay, they do so with the absolute trust that we'll provide them with something much more satisfying than a squirrel. They show us in many ways that sitting and staying present in the moment is not complacency or apathy, but a focused discipline and art that we can all learn together.

You'll get *Instant Insights* on ...

- You can learn to meditate with ease and joy, and if you already meditate, your practice can become one of even more ease and joy.

- You will come to understand that sitting and staying is not passive; it requires a disciplined focus to sit and stay and let all the squirrels of runaway thoughts go by.

- You will learn that practicing this focused discipline not only reduces stress, but that there is no such thing as stress in the moment.

- You will learn how to become more mindfully and heartfully present in the moment.

- You will learn how you can be a compassionate presence for yourself and others, without having to say one word or do one thing other than be here now.

- You will learn that you can witness yourself and others with compassion so that you don't feel the need or desire to engage with all the thoughts that cross your path, and that being present in the moment keeps you free from getting entangled in all the dramas and traumas that the mind can fabricate.

A Gift from the Author

This book is only an introduction to compassionate meditation. As a thank-you for purchasing her book, Sabrina offers you another opportunity to go further into the practice by listening to her audio meditation presentation and guided exercise.

To receive your free audio download, send an e-mail with the word "GIFT" typed in the subject line to the following address:

corporatecompassionista@gmail.com

Dedicated Introduction

My Beloved Teacher, Merlot (1993-2007)

Meditation looks deceptively easy and simple. Simple, yes. Easy? Well, let's just say that for many, it isn't so easy to sit still in complete silence with the only intention being to focus on watching the breath. That's why doing meditation is called "practice." It takes practice just like any other discipline that is learned over time. While it's not necessarily the easiest practice, it does allow for props to help make it not so challenging. Much like when someone new to yoga is given blocks to help prop them up, I'll share some insights with you to help you with your practice—starting with what I learned from my favorite teacher.

I believe the greatest teachers are those who show us how to open the door and enter that schoolroom within each of us that has all the questions and answers. They do this not by telling us how or even by showing us, but by being present with us—perhaps every so often giving us a gentle nudge to go this way or an encouraging smile to let us know we are right where we're supposed to be. The best teachers join us as the best learners. My dog Merlot, a Chardonnay-colored German shepherd–Chow mix, was such a teacher.

Merlot taught me how to sit and stay, something we both learned as we went for walks in my neighborhood, which happens to have an abundance of squirrels. When a squirrel would cross our path, he'd want to chase after it, but upon my command to sit, he would do so. As he sat watching the squirrel go by, I could feel the tension through my hold on the leash, which only increased when I then told him to stay. I not only felt this strain on the leash, but I could see his muscles quiver as he sat watching all the squirrels get away.

This was very much like my first year of learning how to meditate. It took everything in me not to chase after the squirrels of thought that zipped across my mind as I sat with my only intent being to watch the breath. I could feel my body tremor as I sat still and let the thoughts go by, especially the one that said, "Get up and go." But no matter what, I stayed until the ten-minute timer went off.

Preface

A Suggestion Before You Start Reading

This is not a typical "how-to" book. Although I do give some specific instructions, I do not give many directives. That said, I start off with a suggestion of how to use this book most effectively: First, read through all of it. Then go back and read it again, stopping to do the exercises along the way. You may want to have a journal nearby to jot down notes or insights as they come to you. But this is not about journaling, so if you find any kind of writing distracts you from your meditation, then don't write. Read through this book as many times as you need to, as you learn how to sit and stay.

Table of Contents

Why Meditate?

You may wonder, why go through all of this? What's so wrong with chasing squirrels—maybe even catching a few? Nothing at all is wrong ... and nothing is right either. (I'll expand on this later.) It all comes down to what you want, but there's a disclaimer here as well, which you'll find later. First, I want to tell you why I was drawn to the practice.

I was in my first semester of a four-year credentialed program to become a licensed counselor when I came to a point that I thought I could either excel in this new vocation with roaring success or I could fail with a crashing thud. I was terrified of both scenarios because I believed that they were beyond my control. It all depended on what others deemed my fate to be. I'd heard everything from "You've got the gift, babe," to "Here's a card for a really good therapist," and I took it all in as being true about me because "they" said so.

As part of my training, I saw my own counselor on a weekly basis. When I came to her with this crisis, she asked me, "Do you have a meditation practice?" I beamed with pride as I told her, "Yes! I sit in the same chair every morning, in the quiet, and I close my eyes and don't think." She nodded and said, "That's not meditation, at least not mindfulness or insight meditation, or what's known in the Buddhism tradition as Vipassana." I was crushed to find out that what I thought I'd been doing as meditation wasn't, and I was confused by all this terminology of "mindfulness," "insight meditation," and "Vis" something or another. But because I wanted to get out of my predicament, I was willing to give it a try.

My counselor went on to tell me that basically we're always thinking and so there was no "not thinking." She said that meditation teaches us how to be aware of what we're thinking, and then to be mindful of how we respond to such thoughts. This didn't make any sense to me, but it didn't matter because she concluded by saying, "And then, you won't feel as if you're swinging on this pendulum of going from high to low, all dependent on influences outside your control, especially that of other people. ... You'll feel some equilibrium." Now that sounded like something I wanted.

She then explained that mindfulness meditation wasn't about "seeking nirvana"—or seeking anything. It was about sitting in quiet stillness and watching the breath. I told her it sounded boring. She agreed. "Yes," she said, "It's not the sexy fireworks of grandstand visions, or the magical allure of levitation, but as you continue to do this practice every day, you'll see things shift. It seems gradual, but all the same it shifts. You'll see yourself and how you show up in the world in a new way. It's changed my life dramatically for the better." She then topped off this enticing offering with: "And, after spending some dedicated time with the practice, you'll most likely get some valuable insights. That's why it's sometimes called 'insight meditation.'"

Your Instant Insights...

- Mindfulness meditation is not "not thinking." This can't happen because we're always thinking, but we can focus our mind on one thing and that is on watching the breath.

- Mindfulness meditation is about becoming aware of what we're thinking, and then mindfully choosing how we respond. This allows for some equilibrium as we no longer frantically chase after every squirrel of thought that runs across our mind's path.

- Mindfulness meditation isn't about seeking anything. It's about being fully present in the moment so that you feel a sense of connection with yourself and others that opens you to deepening awareness and new insights.

Right Now, Right Now
There Is No Stress

Chasing Squirrels Is Stressful

Until my counselor pointed it out to me, I wasn't even aware that my emotional and mental states swung so wildly up and down. I had no clue that my thoughts were these squirrels that I was forever frantically chasing, but never catching. I didn't know this because I wasn't aware of much of anything when it came to my thoughts and feelings. How could I be? I was too distracted, trying to catch those squirrels of anxious, fearful, worrying thoughts, fueled by the false belief that once I caught them, I could have some peace. But after a few months of meditation, I learned that the peace I so longed for was at hand, waiting for me, once I became still and present in the moment.

If There Is No Past and If There Is No Future, Then What Is There?

When I'm thinking about something that hasn't happened yet, I'm in the future. When I'm thinking about something that has already happened, I'm in the past. Living life in the past or in the future can be stressful. But when we live in the moment, there is no stress. When we understand this, we come to realize that there's no such thing as stress reduction because there's nothing to reduce.

No matter how hard we try, we can't undo anything that has already been done, but if we believe we can and if we focus our energy on doing so, then we're not living in the present and we're causing ourselves undue stress. As for the future, we know we can do many things to prepare for what might happen, yet no matter how much we prepare, certain things are out of our control. This is one of the blessings of living in California with its earthquakes: we learn on a primal level how much is not within our control, no matter how fastidious we may be making sure it looks like everything is.

The Power of Choice

I do have power though, the power of choice, when I am in the moment. Right here and now I can choose how to respond to what is present before me. When I realize this power of choice, I am liberated from the shackles of stress. This is true for all of us, even if we don't always respond in a way that we'd like to. Simply recognizing that we do have a choice of how to respond gives us a sense of freedom from feeling stuck in old patterns of reacting to who or what is yanking our leash ... I mean, "chain."

Sometimes though I want to engage with a past memory, and so I consciously choose to do so, maybe savoring a sweet moment shared with a loved one. Sometimes I want to engage with thoughts about the future, or what I call "a fantasy." At one job, I used to spend part of my lunchtime in a conference room that looked out directly into the Hollywood Hills with the iconic white letters spelled out over the landscape. I'd set a timer for fifteen minutes and daydream while looking out at this view.

There are times, however, when I'm strolling along, pushing my cart at Target, and I see some toy. Suddenly I'm thinking about how I never played with that toy as a child, and then I'm thinking of how I never did this or that as a child. Before I know it, I'm no longer at Target but somewhere off in the distant past, ruminating about all of those seeming deprivations. We need to consciously choose what we wish to engage in, and how we wish to engage with it. The awareness of what we are thinking and feeling comes over time as we learn how to be fully present with our daily meditation practice.

But Aren't There Other Ways to Be Present?

Yes, there are other ways to be fully present in the flow of the moment. For some, it's exploring nature's trails; for others, it's painting or singing or cooking; for still others, it's dancing. It doesn't matter what it is, just so long as it keeps you fully engaged in being present while doing your thing—without focusing on results. Meditation is my thing; it brings me back to being present in the flow, which feels peacefully centering. Be open to discovering what is "your thing" that brings you back home to a centered peace.

Your Instant Insights...

- Chasing after every thought can be stressful, especially so if you believe that once you catch troublesome thoughts (such as worry, fear, anxiety), you'll feel at peace. But peace only comes with letting those thoughts come and go and staying present in the moment.

- Living in the past or future and trying to change what has happened or what may happen causes stress. When we live in the present moment, however, there is no such thing as stress.

- In this moment now, we have the power of choice: we can choose how to respond to what is present before us.

Mindfulness Meditation and Compassion

What Is Mindfulness Meditation?

There are many other ways to meditate; mindfulness is only one. In fact, when I visited some Buddhist monasteries in Thailand, the monks told me they do not consider the Buddhist practice of "Vipassana" (what Western culture calls "mindfulness meditation") to be meditation; rather, they see it as a focusing exercise used to prepare the mind for meditation. For our purposes, however, I am calling this "mindfulness meditation."

As I've said, it's simple: You sit still in a quiet place, close your eyes, and watch the breath. As I also mentioned, it's not all that easy, for you'll notice things that will distract you from this.

You'll notice thoughts and feelings that you'll want to engage with, or you may experience physical sensations, such as itching or tenseness. You gently acknowledge these distractions— but nothing more than that—as you go back to focusing on the breath.

One of my favorite analogies is that of sitting at a train station. When I sit to meditate, it's as though I am sitting on a bench at a train station where I can watch the trains come and go. I sit and watch all these trains of thought come and go, but I don't engage with them. In other words, I stay seated with my focus on watching the breath, and I don't get on the trains. I let them go and continue to sit and stay.

Heartfulness

But what happens when (as I can promise you it will) you're sitting and watching the trains of thought come and go, and you suddenly find yourself on a train headed for Chicago? Wait a minute! How did that happen? Only minutes ago, you were sitting on a bench at a train station in Los Angeles, watching the breath, and ... now? It's called being human.

We are made to think, with beautiful minds that are always thinking. So how do we stop thinking? We don't. We don't stop thinking. That's not the purpose of mindfulness meditation. The purpose is to be mindfully present in the moment by watching the breath, so what happens when we don't do that? We gently bring our attention back to the breath.

Meditation master Jack Kornfield uses the example of house training a puppy. You tell the puppy to use the mat, but the puppy doesn't use the mat. Then you lovingly bring the puppy back to the mat. You do this over and over again, ever so patient, ever so lovingly. This is how we treat ourselves as we gently step off the runaway train and bring ourselves back to the bench. This is heartfulness. Just as puppies respond to love, so do we. We use our practice to learn how to treat ourselves with compassionate, loving kindness as we watch ourselves stray and then gently bring ourselves back to the mat.

Your Instant Insights...

- Mindfulness meditation is simple, but not necessarily easy, for we can get distracted from our focused intent of watching the breath.

- When distractions call our attention, we do not engage with them; instead, we gently acknowledge them and go back to watching the breath.

- We treat ourselves with compassionate, loving kindness when we stray from our focus of watching the breath.

Before We Start to Meditate, Let's Begin with This

Beginner's Mind and Beginner's Heart

"Beginner's Mind" is a Buddhist term, and it means being present and seeing everything in the moment as if it is all new to you. When one of my counseling clients was feeling discouraged about the seeming lackluster state of her marriage, I offered her "Beginner's Mind" to help bring some freshness to the relationship. I suggested that every time she saw her husband, to see him as though she had never seen him before that very moment. I told her that although she had in fact seen him many times before, she had not really seen him in that very specific instant in that very particular way.

She tried it and came back to tell me that she was learning to not only see her husband in a new way, but she was also seeing herself in a new way. She realized she was now present with an open heart, a Beginner's Heart, and there was now some sizzle. As she told it: "It's as though I'm with a new man I've never been with before, moment by moment, and I'm curious because I want to know him." A Beginner's Mind and Heart are joyfully curious because everything is new—and wondrous.

When I teach my group meditation classes, the first thing I tell them is that I've set up a designated space in the parking lot where they can leave every thought they've had before walking into the studio. I promise that if they want, they can pick up those same thoughts when they leave. This way they can start off the class with Beginner's Mind and Beginner's Heart. I then ask them to enter the room as if they've never been there before, even if they have; to look at the people in the room as if they've never seen them before, even if they have. I ask them to be present in the moment, as if this moment has never been before or will be again as it is now.

Exercise:
Opening the Door to Beginner's Mind

I can't offer you a designated parking spot, but I have this suggestion: Close your eyes and imagine yourself standing outside the door of the room you're in right now. Imagine this spot as being one long, wide, endless hallway where you can let go of all your thoughts, opinions, and beliefs, for there is unlimited space to contain them. Keeping your eyes closed, imagine placing your hand on the doorknob of this room that you've never been in before and turning it. Slowly open the door, keeping your eyes closed, and stand still for a moment. Now open your eyes. Surprise! You're now in a new place you've never been before until this very moment. When you leave, you may go back out the same door into the same hallway and collect everything you left there.

The One and Only "Rule": There Is No Right; There Is No Wrong

> *"Beyond our ideas of right-doing and wrong-doing, there is a field. I'll meet you there."*
>
> – Rumi

After introducing my class to Beginner's Mind and Beginner's Heart, I tell them that there is only one rule in my class, and it's the only rule you'll find in this book: There is no right, and there is no wrong. If you fall asleep, it's okay. If you mentally balance your checkbook, it's okay. This is your meditation practice, and how you choose to engage with it is up to you. If you choose to make yourself "wrong" or "right" as to how you meditate ... well, that's your choice, and it's not a wrong or a right choice.

Just as there's no "right" or "wrong," there's also no "good" or "bad." You may say that you're "good" or "bad" at meditation, but really it's that you *feel* good or bad about your practice. To use words without quite so much judgment, you might describe your meditation practice as "pleasant" or "unpleasant."

The important thing is that you just do it. Designate a specific amount of time each day to meditate, and do it without judgment about whether it's right or wrong, good or bad. As we start to honor this "rule" of no right and no wrong, we begin to live with compassion for ourselves and for others. We learn how to be gentle and kind with ourselves as to how we choose to engage in our practice, and in life.

Your Instant Insights...

- We can choose to see and to be present with Beginner's Mind and Beginner's Heart so that everything and everyone is all new to us, for we have not seen what we are seeing now, or felt what we are feeling now, in this very instant at this moment.

- Beginner's Mind and Beginner's Heart invite us to be joyfully curious as we watch what presents itself in this very moment.

- There is only one "rule" when it comes to meditation, and really to all of life, which is this: There is no right; there is no wrong. It's your practice, as it is your life, and how you choose to engage with it is your choice—so long as you don't hurt yourself or anyone else.

Preparing to Sit

Silence

"You haven't partied until you've partied at dawn in complete silence with Buddhist monks."

– Cameron Diaz

Mindfulness meditation is done in silence, or in as silent a spot as you can find. Some people enjoy playing relaxing music as they meditate, or having someone speak to them as a guided meditation, but there is power in silence. Sitting in quiet stillness, we give ourselves the time and space that we usually don't have during our daily activities when smartphones are bleeping, dinging, and ringing every time we get a message; when music is blasting in many stores and restaurants; and with the ceaseless cacophony of city traffic with alarms going off and sirens blaring.

I know this for sure: We crave silence.

A few years ago, I taught my meditation class to a group of fourteen teenagers. I asked them to raise their hand if in the past twenty-four hours they'd experienced some silence. Only two raised their hands. I then asked how many wanted some silent time. All of them immediately raised their hands. We intuitively know that we need silence to replenish our souls and rest our minds, and so we crave it when we don't get it.

I'll repeat myself again: there is no right, and there is no wrong. If you feel as though you can't sit still in total silence, there are sound machines with recordings of waves or other sounds of nature that you might find helpful. When I first started to sit, I used my neighbor's sprinklers that were on a timer for ten minutes every morning as my background noise.

How to Sit

If you're sitting in a chair, make sure you're sitting with your back straight so that there's no slouching, but your posture shouldn't be rigid. Place your feet flat on the floor, spread out to about hip width so that you feel comfortable. Your shoulders should be relaxed and open, with your upper arms resting against your torso and your forearms bent ever so slightly to allow you to rest both hands on your lap, palms up.

If you're sitting on the floor or on a cushion, sit with your back straight but not rigid. In whatever position you sit, whether it be the lotus position or whether you use a stool to help support you as you kneel, you should feel comfortable. Just like those who sit in a chair, relax your shoulders, and rest your upper arms against your torso. Bend your forearms ever so slightly to allow your hands to rest on your lap, palms up. Your head should be upright; be careful that it isn't tilted too far forward or backward.

Eyes Closed

There are other types of mindfulness meditations where we keep the eyes open, such as walking, eating, or contemplation. But for sitting meditation, we close our eyes. Don't squeeze your eyes tight, but softly close them. If you don't feel comfortable closing your eyes, then lower your gaze downward to the floor space in front of you.

How to Breathe
Focus Is on *Watching* the Breath –
Not on Breathing

Breathe through the nose, mouth closed, with your tongue gently placed against your bottom teeth. This isn't like yoga, where the emphasis is on using the breath to help body movement, so there are no deep inhales and exhales. You breathe just like you are breathing now while reading this. And just like you breathe throughout the day, occasionally you may take in a deeper breath, but still breathe through the nose with the mouth closed.

The focus of mindfulness meditation is on watching the breath, not on the actual breathing. As you watch the breath move through your body, notice how it feels. It might feel warm as it moves out through the nostrils, or it might feel forced or maybe relaxed. You'll notice how each breath is different. Some breaths are long and drawn out; some are short. Some breaths are shallow; some are deep.

In ... Out

To help keep your focus on the breath, silently say "in" to yourself every time you breathe in and "out" when you breathe out. However, the focus isn't on saying "in" and "out" with each inhale and exhale; this is only a tool to help you keep your attention on the breath.

Your Instant Insights...

- Meditate in silence; if you must have background noise, use a sound machine with nature sounds. We need silence to replenish and rest our mind and soul.

- Notice the breath, how it feels as it moves through your body, how each breath is different.

- It's about watching the breath, not about breathing.

What to Do When You Start to Think Something or Hear Something... Or Feel Itchy or Twitchy

We're Always Thinking

I repeat myself because I want you to understand certain basic concepts, and I also want to clear up any misconceptions that you may have had about meditation before reading this book. When my students first start, they have several misunderstandings about meditation. One is that if they don't do it a certain way, it's wrong. Well, that's not so. Another is that the goal of meditation is to "clear the mind" or "empty it of thought" or to "stop thinking." Okay, let's carefully look at these three goals. They all involve a thinking activity—clearing, emptying, stopping. My point is that we are always thinking, on one level or another. Focusing on the breath is a thinking activity, but with this focused intent, we're not so easily distracted. However, if distractions such as thoughts and feelings come up, we don't ignore them. We acknowledge the distractions, but we don't engage with them, and then we go back to the breath.

A Mindfulness Exercise: Counting Squirrels

This first exercise will show you how our mind is always working. It will take all of one minute, but you'll need a timer. (And have this timer ready to use again for your meditations.) Get yourself settled into your sitting posture, set the timer for a minute, and close your eyes; with your mouth closed, breathe through the nose and count your thoughts. Some people think thoughts with words, and some people see their thoughts with images. You might find yourself going, "Hmm ... it's rather quiet," before realizing that's a thought right there! Some people will count eight or ten thoughts, others maybe twenty or even thirty or more. The point of this exercise is that we're always thinking, even if we're not always aware that we are thinking or what we're thinking about. As we continue our meditation practice though, we become ever more aware of our thoughts and more mindful of how we wish to engage with them.

Notice, Note, and Label

As I promised, you'll find yourself meditating and a thought or two or twenty will get your attention so that you're no longer focusing on watching the breath. When this happens, you notice it, but you don't engage with it. You do this by noting the thought with a simple label of "thinking, thinking, thinking." By the time you finish silently repeating the word "thinking" three times, the thought has come and gone, and you can go back to focusing on the breath. You do the same thing if you hear something that catches your attention: notice it and note it by silently repeating the generic label of "hearing, hearing, hearing." If you feel a physical sensation, such as your eye twitching or your hand itching, you notice it and note it with a simple label, such as "twitching, twitching, twitching" or "itching, itching, itching," and you bring your attention back to watching the breath. The simpler the better when it comes to labeling. You don't need a dictionary or thesaurus, and you're not telling a story. You're merely noticing and noting with the simplest label possible.

But what happens if, after you notice and note a thought by labeling it "thinking" and go back to the breath, the same thought comes up again? You do the same thing again: you notice it, note it with the label "thinking, thinking, thinking," and then bring yourself back to the breath. Or what happens if you notice one thought, note it with the label "thinking," go back to the breath, but then immediately notice another thought? You do the same thing: you notice, note, label, and then go back to the breath. What happens if the same thought comes back over and over again? You notice, note, and label over and over again as "thinking." For the first three years of my practice, many of my meditations were what I called—with a great deal of compassion for myself—"thinking meditations."

One thing I noticed early on in my practice was how easy it was to be lulled into believing that I was watching the breath when what I was really doing was thinking. I would be silently saying to myself "in" and "out" with each inhale and exhale, but I'd be doing so all the while in the middle of some thought. Using the analogy of watching trains, it was as though I believed I was still sitting on the bench watching trains, but I'd find myself on a train to Chicago. This still happens, but I notice it more quickly and smile at myself with tender compassion.

Your Instant Insights...

- We are always thinking. The intent of mindfulness meditation is not to stop thinking.

- The intent of mindfulness meditation is to focus on watching the breath; to acknowledge any thoughts and feelings that catch our attention, but not engage with them.

- It is easy to believe we are watching the breath as we silently repeat "in" and "out," but what we are really doing is thinking; before we know it, we're on a runaway train of thought.

Your First Sit and Stay

Now that you know how to sit, how to breathe, and how to notice and note distractions, you're ready for your first meditation. Even if you've been meditating for years, I invite you to treat this as your first sit with Beginner's Mind and Heart. If you are new and this is your first time, then I also invite you to do so with Beginner's Mind and Heart, being open to and curious about what presents itself to you each moment as you sit in quiet stillness watching the breath.

You'll set the timer for five minutes, but before you do, there are a few instructions for when the timer goes off. First, keeping your eyes closed and breathing through the mouth, take in a few deep breaths. Then slowly open your eyes and gently bring your attention back to the room with your body still for a few more seconds. Next, take note of how you feel now and how you felt while meditating. Notice if anything repeatedly called your attention during your sit. If there were any repeated distractions that you can change or adjust, such as turning off a noisy air conditioner or shutting a window so that outside noise is muted, then do so now. Finally, walk around the room for a few minutes while shaking your hands a bit and softly rotating your shoulders, perhaps doing a little hip wiggly-wiggly.

NOW you're all prepared and ready for your first sit. Set the timer and let's go!

And Repeat

After you've finished walking and stretching a bit from your first sit, come back to your seat and prepare for another five-minute sit. As before, when the timer goes off, you'll gently bring your attention back to the room, notice how you feel, take note of anything outstanding that called to you during your sit ... and give yourself a big hug of congratulations for having completed two five-minute sits! Yay you!!

And Repeat Again, and Again ...
It's Called Practice, Practice, Practice

Now, put this book away for a few hours before repeating another set of two five-minute sits, or maybe wait until the end of the day to meditate again. Maybe the next day repeat two sits in the morning and two in the evening. Build up to one ten-minute sit when you feel ready—only you will know when you're ready. You might even start with a ten-minute sit, especially if you already have a meditation practice.

With this daily sit and stay, you now have a meditation practice! Practice with dedication, and the length of your sit will increase. I sit for thirty to forty-five minutes in the morning, but it has taken over eleven years to get to this point.

Your Instant Insights...

- You can meditate!

- Only you know what feels right for you as to how long and how often you wish to meditate, but meditate at least once a day—twice if you can.

- CONGRATS and yay you! Give yourself a big high five!

Some Props and Pointers to Help You Continue Your Practice

Listen to Your Beautiful Body

"The body says what words cannot."

– Martha Graham

When we sit to meditate, we sit in quiet stillness. Sitting still allows us not only to rest the body, but it also allows us to become much more aware of the body. Stillness is to the body what quiet is to the mind. Just as you come to recognize all the activity going on in your beautiful mind, you'll also come to a new understanding of your beautiful body and learn how to listen to what it's telling you. Perhaps you never noticed how tight your shoulders are or the slight burning sensation in your little toe. But as you sit still, you become aware of the body's sensations.

By staying still, you allow yourself to feel these sensations without judgment and without the need to do anything about them other than notice them. You don't engage with the sensations. You notice the itch, but you don't scratch it. You notice the tightness (almost to the point of cramping) in your calf muscle, but you don't stretch out your leg to relieve it. You notice the burning in your little toe, but you don't tell yourself that's what happens when you wear shoes that look good but are too tight. You continue to sit still, and with Beginner's Mind and Beginner's Heart you're open to and curious about what happens as you stay present in the stillness. You'll soon realize that the body is a treasure chest of information about your physical, emotional, and mental states, and about your soul, for it is the temple that embodies it.

Again, there's no right, and there's no wrong. If you're meditating and feel a charley horse in your leg—unlike any cramp you've experienced before—then stretch out your leg and note this by labeling it "stretching." But I encourage you, if you can, to stay still and be present with the sensation. The one thing you'll learn early on when you start your practice is that everything changes, always, moment by moment. That cramp will eventually go away. You'll probably forget about it, and with your new awareness, you'll be surprised by how quickly you've forgotten about it. But if you stay still and present with it and watch it come and go, you might get some insight into what the cramp is about. Maybe it's something as simple as "drink more water"; maybe it's something else, such as your body trying to adjust itself to being still and not overriding the sensation with activity. Simply remember that the focus is always on watching the breath and noticing what distracts you from it, not engaging with it. Yet in being still, you become aware of those thoughts that your body cannot express in words.

Be Consistent with Your Practice

Your practice is most beneficial if you can meditate at the same time and same place every day. I have a designated meditation chair that I sit in, and I do my practice in the morning before I start my day and end it by sitting in this same chair with a few minutes of meditation. Consistently showing up, no matter what is going on in my life, has been the key to my practice. This consistency, however, has its own variances, for one of the things that I first learned from meditating is that nothing stays the same. That said, I may meditate later in the morning on a weekend when I sleep in, or I may meditate during my lunch hour in an empty conference room if I leave home earlier than usual for an appointment before work. It's doesn't look the same every day, but it's still consistent. And remember: there is no right or wrong.

The ideal is to start and end your day with meditation. For me, however, meditating at night has been a challenge. When I first started, I tried to sit at night and meditate, but I felt as if a thousand ants were crawling all over me. It felt like torture. When I talked to my counselor about this, she told me that there were other ways to practice mindfulness, one of which is Tai Chi. I signed up for a weekly Tai Chi class and practiced my steps each night before I went to bed as my meditation to end the day. A year ago, I noticed that it was becoming more challenging for me to do my longer mediation in the morning, so I changed my routine. Instead of exercising after my meditation, I now exercise before, which helps me relax. Again, there's no right way, and there's no wrong way; there is only your way. But whatever you choose, dedicating a certain time and place each day for your meditation is part of the consistency that builds your practice so that it becomes an integral part of your self-care routine.

Your Instant Insights...

- Sitting in quiet stillness allows you to listen to what your body is telling you.

- The body is a treasure trove of information about your physical, emotional, mental states.

- Be consistent with your practice, making a dedicated commitment to meditate at the same time and place at least once during your day.

Don't Stop

Do Not Stop Meditating – Part 1

No Matter How Genius It Is, Do Not Stop to Write It Down

The mind has a sneaky way of getting our attention while we're focused on watching the breath: it gives us thunderbolts of genius ideas. I mean so Genuinely Genius that you feel you must stop your meditation and write them down or you'll lose them.

But don't.

Don't stop meditating. Acknowledge the genius idea; notice it and note it by labeling it the same as any other thought with "thinking, thinking, thinking." Then go back to focusing on the breath. When you finish your sit, you can write down the

Genuinely Genius idea. If you can't remember it, then it wasn't Genuinely Genius. Maybe you'll remember it while you're washing dishes or on the treadmill—then it is Genuinely Genius.

When I first started my practice, I was tempted to fall prey to these genius ideas. Even though I didn't stop meditating to write them down, I wanted to see how many genius ideas I could collect in one sit, all the while noting and labeling these ideas as "thinking." With a burst of enthusiasm for all the ideas I was getting, I told this to my counselor. She reminded me that the one and only focus of meditation is to watch the breath and, by doing so, to be present in the moment.

After that, I found myself watching one genius idea after another pass on by while I continued to focus on the breath. Every so often I would start to engage with one of the geniuses, and when I became aware of this, I found myself noticing it and noting it with the label that described my emotional state at that moment, such as "wanting, wanting, wanting." I wanted to play with the geniuses; it was so much more fun than watching the breath.

Do Not Stop Meditating – Part 2

Not So Genius, but Just as Powerfully Alluring

The other kind of thinking that may pull at your attention so strongly that you feel you must stop meditating to take care of it are questions of doubt—not deep, philosophical questions of doubt, but tiny, nagging doubts that eat at you like a mosquito bite. "Did I turn off the burner under the soup pot? I'm not sure—I'd better stop and check." "Did I lock the front door? I can't remember. Hmm ... I'd better stop and check." Treat these doubts like any other thoughts by noticing and noting them with the generic label of "thinking." Once you finish meditating you can go check on all these things, but most likely you won't feel as much urgency to do so as you did during your sit.

Focused Intention Is All That Is Required

If you're engaging in a meditation practice, it must have some importance to you because you are devoting your time and attention to it. To have the intention to sit still and stay present in the quiet with your focused attention on the breath is all that is required. When we tell a dog to "sit and stay" and the dog starts to squirm, we may notice the tentative wiggling of the behind, but we don't get caught up in telling the dog to stay completely still. We may, however, give a reminder to "staaaaay," and that's what we do for ourselves.

We don't judge ourselves if we fidget, but we remind ourselves that our intention is to stay focused on the breath. So we notice and note the fidgeting with a simple label, such as "fidgeting" or perhaps "restlessness," and then we go back to the breath.

Being Focused Is Being Heart-Centered

The Latin root of "focus" is "hearth." When we are focused on something, whether it's watching the breath or creating a piece of art or completing a work project, we are hearth or heart-centered. When we are focused in the flow of the moment, we are listening to our heart—our own inner guru—and following where it leads us.

Getting to this point of laser focus, however, takes practice. That's why I encourage you to sit and stay as you note and label distractions and to stay present with the way such distractions feel when they catch your attention. It's not engaging with the distractions; it's being fully aware of and attuned to how they affect you—your body, mind, and emotions. You notice the feelings, but in the same way as you notice the breath: by watching them as they move through your body. With this deeper level of awareness, you become less engaged with the mind and all its busyness. You're listening to your body, and you'll soon realize the command center of your body is your heart.

This concentrated focus is a stillness, whether you're meditating or hiking a mountain, that allows you to be present from your heart. When we are heart-centered, the mind doesn't get in the way with its detours of thought. When we are present with an open heart, we have a wise understanding that clearly sees and knows the next step to take, moment by moment. This is heartfulness.

Your Instant Insights...

- Do not stop meditating. If you get a genius idea, you'll remember it when you finish. Do not stop meditating to see if you turned off the stove or locked the door; you can check on this when you finish. Do note and label these distractions as "thinking," and go back to watching the breath.

- All that is required is that you have a focused intention to watch the breath. That's it. If you fidget or itch or go to sleep, it's okay. But notice and note this with a simple label, such as "fidgeting" or "sleeping," and then go back to the breath.

- When we are focused in being present in the moment, we are heart-centered and can listen to our heart—our own inner guru.

You Know Your Meditation Is Working When...

It Gets Louder

As I said in the first chapter, if you continue to read, you'll find a disclaimer about how meditation "comes down to what you want." Here's the disclaimer: My story is that I was looking for some peace of mind and balance, but that's not what I got—at first. No, not at all. After a few months of meditating, I told my counselor, "This meditation thing isn't working." She asked why I felt this way, and I said, "It's like there's a radio playing in my head that's been turned up to full volume." She said, "Ah, but that means it is working." This was not what I wanted. She then explained, "That radio has been playing in your head all along, but you were too distracted by other things, so you never noticed it. But now you're paying attention to what you're thinking and to how you're feeling, so it just feels like it's getting louder."

Many years later, it can still occasionally feel as if a radio is blasting in my head or like a million different stations are playing at the same time, but my daily practice has taught me how to stop and pause ... which is another way to say "sit and stay." I do this even though I'm not sitting and meditating, but I follow the same pattern as if I am: I notice and note the thoughts, but I don't engage with them. Instead, I take in a few deep breaths and pay attention to how it feels as the breath moves through me. I may do this stop-and-pause a few times until it feels like there's not quite so much radio activity. This pause allows me to become more consciously aware of what I'm thinking, and as a result, I can change the channel—and the volume.

It Feels Bombarding

As I said, it can sometimes feel as if there are a million radio stations playing in my head all at the same time, or it may feel as if there's an itch and a twitch and so many thoughts and so many sounds all coming at me at the same time—and this may be. But I know that no matter how fast my beautiful mind may process one thought after another, in the moment I can pay attention to only one thing, one sound, one sensation. The focus it takes to notice and note one distraction among a seeming cacophony comes with years of practice.

Feelings Pop Up

A few months after I started meditating, I noticed something such as this: I'd be driving home after work, thinking about something relatively mundane, such as doing laundry or some other chore. I'd be aware of this thought as "planning," which is at the top of my list of enjoyable thinking activities, but suddenly I could feel my jaw clench, which was my body telling me something about my emotions. It was anger, which confused me. Why was I feeling anger about laundry?

I wasn't engaging with it, but I was watching myself feel it and was curious. I noticed and noted the anger, but I also allowed myself to feel the anger as it moved through my body and tensed the muscles—and then I got an instant insight! I was feeling angry because I believed I'd done enough work for the day, and I didn't want to go home to more work of laundry. Although it seemed as if the anger came out of nowhere, it hadn't. But now, I was more aware of the thoughts that led up to it and, more importantly, how I could change that line of thinking and feeling if I wanted to.

Again, the intention of a meditation practice is not to seek and find, but to be open and present while "sitting on the cushion" meditating—and off the cushion as well. With increased mindfulness in all we do, we become more awake to our inner wisdom.

Your Instant Insights...

- Practicing mindfulness mediation, we start to become aware of thought patterns and feelings that may be seem uncomfortable and unpleasant.

- When this happens outside our meditation, we can sit and stay by giving ourselves a few minutes to stop and pause. We do this by taking in a few deep breaths and paying attention to how it feels as the breath moves through the body.

- By watching thoughts and feelings and not engaging with them, we are open and receptive to invaluable insights about ourselves that we can use to change how we think and feel.

And Then What?

We Do Not Take Possession

Did you notice when I shared my story about angry laundry, I did not say "my anger" but rather "anger" or "the anger"? This is what we learn to do as we notice and note our thoughts and feelings by labeling them with generics, and then let them pass on by while we go back to the breath. When we don't take possession of thoughts and feelings, we don't take on their labels.

Going back to the laundry, you'll see I don't say, "I am angry," but rather "I am *feeling* angry." I do not identify myself by the feeling I am experiencing or the thought that I am thinking. This is key to being able to open ourselves to experiencing unpleasant feelings and then to letting it go as we stay fully present. If we feel uncomfortable with thoughts and feelings that get our attention, the temptation is to mull over the circumstance or situation that was the seeming prompt for those feelings; when we do that, however, we're no longer mindfully or heartfully present, but rather in the past.

Clearing Possession, There's Some Space

By not taking possession of feelings and thoughts, we are not invested in what happens or doesn't happen. We allow some space, some breathing room, for all that's going on inside and outside us, and then we're not so attached to it. This is not apathy. No, rather it's a level of engagement where we do not feel compelled to take action in order to change someone or something that feels uncomfortable.

This space gives us a new perspective. It's like when we peer through a microscope, we see only one cell, but when we stand back and allow for some space between us and what we're looking at, we see the image of that one cell within many cells much differently. Giving ourselves some space doesn't mean that we will not feel uncomfortable, but rather we will have a more expansive view and see the discomfort within a bigger picture. This is what I call witnessing. We are witnessing the feelings and thoughts we are experiencing within the spaciousness of the heart rather than in the circumscribed boundaries of the mind.

In the Space of the Heart

As I said before, my first few years of practice consisted of "thinking meditations" with most of the time spent noticing and noting thoughts, especially planning. There were many mornings when I noted the breath so that with each inhale and exhale I'd silently say "planning, planning," and not "in, out." When I recognized what I was doing, I'd start to judge myself and note that with "judging, judging, judging," before going back to watching the breath. This pattern would repeat itself again and again. But by not taking possession of the incessant thinking or the subsequent judging, I didn't feel as if I was meditating "wrong" or that I was somehow "not getting it." No, I knew I was getting it, and that right now that was "it."

There came a morning during one of my "thinking meditations," however, when I heard a little voice within me. It sounded like a loving parent whose child wants them to read the same bedtime story over again, and it seems as if the child will not tire and fall asleep. After the third reading, the parent might gently ask, "Are we done now?" Hearing and feeling the tenderness of this voice made me smile. I realized in that moment that I was the child and the parent and that there was no judgment, only loving kindness. This was the voice of my own compassionate witness.

Your Instant Insights...

- By not claiming thoughts and feelings as "my" or "mine," we do not identify ourselves with them; rather, we are open to being fully present as we watch ourselves experience them as they come and go.

- By not taking possession of thoughts and feelings, we clear space that allows us to live in the expansiveness of the heart, which knows only the present moment.

- Being heartfully present, we welcome our own compassionate witness.

We Witness, with Compassion

After the first visit by my compassionate witness, I realized that this loving kindness had always been within me, but I had not allowed it to make itself known. I'd been too busy getting entangled with thoughts, fabricating webs of dramas and traumas. But now I was watching thoughts come and go, as well as judgment and anything else that came my way, while being mindfully present. The heart doesn't live or breathe in the past or future, only in the now.

This was what I learned with on-the-job training. I'd been working for the same company and boss for over ten years and wasn't happy. Then I started meditating, and everything changed— or rather, I changed and my view of everything, and consequently how I experienced everything, changed. I came to see how much drama I created by getting entangled with lines of thinking and the resulting stories that I invented and believed without any evidence of fact. But once I started to notice and note the thoughts that called my attention, I didn't feel the need to engage with them. I could let them go and let go of the fictitious truths that caused so much emotional turbulence and stress.

Many times during these first few years of my practice, I'd witness myself and feel a mix of surprise, befuddlement, and joy. I knew it was me that I was witnessing, but it was me in a way I had never known myself before to act, feel, or think. Instead of taking my boss's grumblings about a client or work situation personally, I'd pause and listen with an open heart and then respond with a soft "Oh ..." Sometimes it was an "Ah ...," or if it called for it, perhaps a "Whoa ..."

By witnessing on the job, I was learning compassion for myself and my boss. Realizing I couldn't say or do anything that would change how he felt, I didn't take on the burden of having to do anything. I simply witnessed, with compassion. This was the true peace I longed for when I first started learning to meditate, but it was more. It was freedom from feeling and believing that I had to do something for someone else so that I could feel at peace with them—and with myself. I could literally let it be. (FYI: Over time, my boss and I became good friends.)

Your Instant Insights...

- The ultimate "sit and stay" is to let it be. When we can allow what passes before us to be as it is, whether it's squirrels of thought or cranky bosses, and witness without judgment or commentary, we are letting it be.

- To witness with an open heart is about as close to unconditional love that we as humans may experience.

- We may never be able to truly master unconditional love as our beloved pets have, but we can show up as a compassionate presence.

About the Author

For a large part of her career, Sabrina Johnson has simultaneously had two vocations: one being her "paycheck job" as an executive assistant for some of the leading players in the entertainment field, and the other her "passion work" as a licensed counselor seeing clients one-on-one as well as creating and facilitating workshops. The convergence of the two has made Sabrina's journey to becoming "The Corporate Compassionista" a seamless one as she shares her compassionate meditation teachings with corporate employees at companies such as Anthem Blue Cross.

Sabrina embarked on this journey in 2005 when she enrolled in a four-year accredited program to become a licensed Practitioner with Centers for Spiritual Living (this is the designation "RScP"). Throughout her training, Sabrina worked with a mindfulness meditation teacher who studied at the Insight Meditation Society under the auspices of its co-founders Jack Kornfield and Joseph Goldsmith. In 2014, Sabrina went on to study Mindfulness Self-Compassion as originated by Kristen Neff, PhD, and Christopher K. Germer. Sabrina then integrated the practice of mindfulness compassion, together with the meditation teachings she had studied, to create and facilitate an eight-week program called "How to be Your Own Compassionate Witness."

Understanding that meditation is a lifelong practice, Sabrina continues to enrich and expand her practice with new adventures, the most recent being an eight-day silent meditation retreat in Hana, Hawaii. Sabrina came back from this retreat with a greater appreciation for how mindfulness, especially when engaged in with an open heart, can help transform those areas of our lives that may appear blocked. This inspired her to start a free support group called Compassionate-Eating. The mission is to come together in community and be compassionate witnesses to one another while dealing with issues of food, weight, body image—all the uncomfortable "elephant in the room" stuff—using compassionate meditation as the foundation for this work. The impetus for this support group was not only Sabrina's desire for greater self-care of body, mind, and spirit, but also to be in community in a new way.

Sabrina learned about community as an essential component of wholeness when she spent two weeks in 2012 mentoring teenage volunteers at The Elephant Sanctuary in Chaing Mai, Thailand. Sabrina witnessed how deeply elephants care for one another as she watched them play together and take care of each other. She saw how they made sure that the blind elephant got her food first, and how they would gently nudge another elephant injured from abuse to help her walk.

A few years ago, Sabrina also found another way to create community on the worldwide web when she co-hosted *The Amazing Hour*, an internet radio show during which she interviewed people who shared their unique talents and gifts to better the world. An amazing thing happened to Sabrina while doing this show: she realized how important it was for her to share her own gifts and talents, one of which is teaching compassionate meditation.

Connect with the Author

Websites:
https://thecorporatecompassionista.com
www.compassionate-eating.com

Email:
corporatecompassionista@gmail.com

Address:
13856 Hamlin Street, Valley Glen, CA 91401

Phone:
(818) 785-9930

Social Media:
LinkedIn:
https://www.linkedin.com/company-beta/16247605

Facebook:
https://www.facebook.com/
thecorporatecompassionista

YouTube:
https://www.youtube.com/channel/
UCGJ5wVXO5g_6fHaOCpaHuDg

About Crescendo Publishing

Crescendo Publishing is a boutique-style, concierge VIP publishing company assisting entrepreneurs with writing, publishing, and promoting their books for the purposes of lead-generation and achieving global platform growth, then monetizing it for even more income opportunities.

Check out some of our latest best-selling
AuthorPreneurs at
http://CrescendoPublishing.com/new-authors

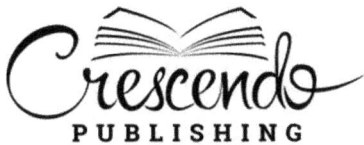

PUBLISHING

About the Instant Insights™ Book Series

The *Instant Insights™ Book Series* is a fact-only, short-read, book series written by EXPERTS in very specialized categories. These high-value, high-quality books can be produced in ONLY 6-8 weeks, from concept to launch, in BOTH PRINT & eBOOK Formats!

This book series is FOR YOU if:

- You are an expert in your niche or area of specialty

- You want to write a book to position yourself as an expert

- You want YOUR OWN book – NOT a chapter in someone else's book

- You want to have a book to give to people when you're speaking at events or simply networking

- You want to have it available quickly

- You don't have the time to invest in writing a 200-page full book

- You don't have a ton of money to invest in the production of a full book – editing, cover design, interior layout, best-seller promotion

- You don't have a ton of time to invest in finding quality contractors for the production of your book – editing, cover design, interior layout, best-seller promotion

For more information on how you can become an

Instant Insights™ author, visit
www.InstantInsightsBooks.com

More Books in the
Instant Insight™ *Series*

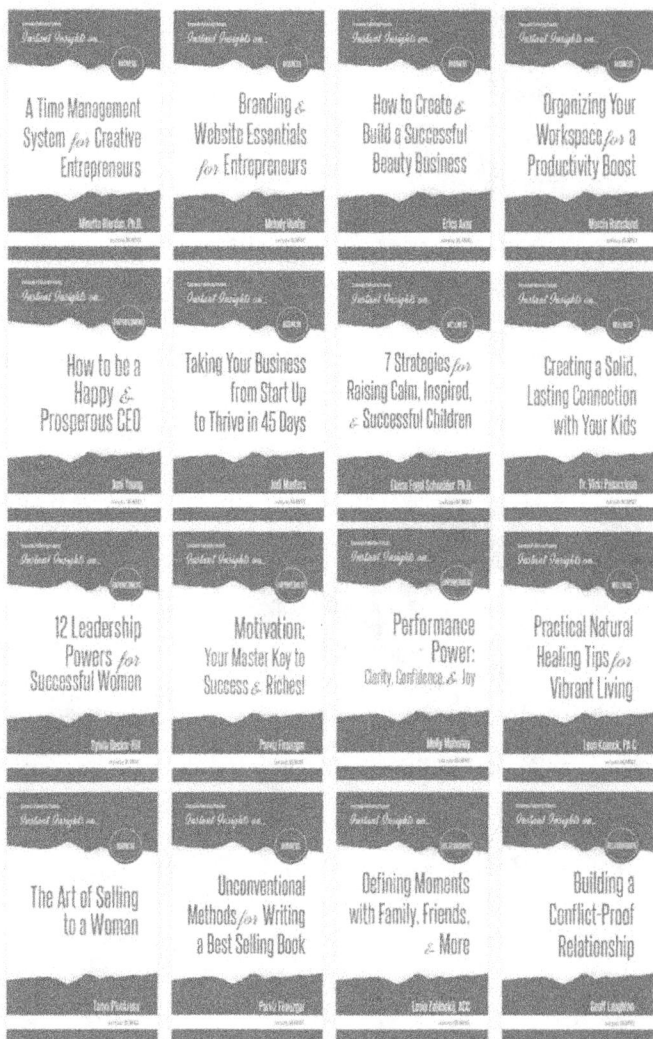

A Time Management System for Creative Entrepreneurs
Minette Riordan, Ph.D.

Branding & Website Essentials for Entrepreneurs
Melody Marks

How to Create & Build a Successful Beauty Business
Erica Avila

Organizing Your Workspace for a Productivity Boost
Marcia Ramsland

How to be a Happy & Prosperous CEO
Josh Young

Taking Your Business from Start Up to Thrive in 45 Days
Andi Manlora

7 Strategies for Raising Calm, Inspired, & Successful Children
Elena Fogel Schneider, Ph.D.

Creating a Solid, Lasting Connection with Your Kids
Dr. Vicki Panaccione

12 Leadership Powers for Successful Women
Cynia Decker-Hill

Motivation: Your Master Key to Success & Riches!
Parviz Firouzgar

Performance Power: Clarity, Confidence, & Joy
Molly Mahoney

Practical Natural Healing Tips for Vibrant Living
Leon Koznick, Ph.C.

The Art of Selling to a Woman
Tania Phillips

Unconventional Methods for Writing a Best Selling Book
Paviz Firouzgar

Defining Moments with Family, Friends, & More
Lynda Zielinski, ACC

Building a Conflict-Proof Relationship
Geoff Laughton

Crescendo
CrescendoPublishing.com

www.ingramcontent.com/pod-product-compliance
Lightning Source LLC
Chambersburg PA
CBHW060516280326
41933CB00014B/2987